Flowchart Smart

The WATER CYCLE

Richard and Louise Spilsbury

Gareth Stevens PUBLISHING

Please visit our website, **www.garethstevens.com**.
For a free color catalog of all our high-quality books,
call toll free 1-800-542-2595 or fax 1-877-542-2596.

Cataloging-in-Publication Data
Names: Spilsbury, Richard. | Spilsbury, Louise.
Title: The water cycle / Richard and Louise Spilsbury.
Description: New York : Gareth Stevens Publishing, 2019. | Series: Flowchart smart | Includes glossary and index.
Identifiers: ISBN 9781538234792 (pbk.) | ISBN 9781538234808 (library bound)
Subjects: LCSH: Hydrologic cycle--Juvenile literature. | Water--Juvenile literature.
Classification: LCC GB662.3 S677 2019 | DDC 551.48--dc23

First Edition

Published in 2019 by
Gareth Stevens Publishing
111 East 14th Street, Suite 349
New York, NY 10003

Produced for Gareth Stevens by Calcium
Editors: Sarah Eason and Harriet McGregor
Designer: Emma DeBanks
Picture researcher: Rachel Blount

Picture credits: Cover: Shutterstock: Denk Creative (br), Visual Generation (c); Inside: Shutterstock: ADfoto: pp. 40–41; AnimalName-Design: p. 31; BGSmith: pp. 1, 6bl; Inna Bigun: p. 11; Chaiyabutra: p. 13; Denk Creative: p. 5br; Designua: pp. 6–7, 12, 26–27, 29; Annalisa e Marina Durante: pp. 8–9; Elroyspelbos: pp. 18–19; Ion George: p. 21tr; Leszek Glasner: p. 17b; Goory: p. 39r; GraphicsRF: p. 15; I love photo: p. 10; Pakenee Kittipinyowat: p. 27t; Kletr: p. 41b; Alexey Kljatov: pp. 20–21; Lumen-digital: p. 30; Makc: p. 43; Marktucan: pp. 24–25; Nikkytok: p. 45t; Anna Nikonorova: p. 19t; Oneshutter Onememory: p. 35t; Phannasit: p. 4b; Pixinoo: pp. 44–45; Suzanna Pratt: p. 33t; Sasa Prudkov: pp. 34–35; Sourav Diaz: pp. 38–39; Stanlonut: p. 25t; Tele52: pp. 32–33; Titus and Co: pp. 16–17; Merkushev Vasiliy: pp. 4–5; Visual Generation: p. 4tr.

Printed in the United States of America

CPSIA compliance information: Batch #CW19GS: For further information contact Gareth Stevens, New York, New York at 1-800-542-2595.

Contents

Chapter 1 **What Is the Water Cycle?......................4**

Chapter 2 **Water in the Atmosphere 10**

Chapter 3 **Water in the Clouds 16**

Chapter 4 **Water Stores 24**

Chapter 5 **Water for Life.....................................30**

Chapter 6 **Using Water..38**

Glossary..46

For More Information 47

Index..48

Chapter 1

What Is the Water Cycle?

The water that you drink today is the same water that was in lakes and rivers when dinosaurs roamed the planet and in the seas where the first fish swam. The water on Earth today is the same water that's been here for 4.6 billion years. It is **recycled** between the planet's surface and the **atmosphere** in the water cycle.

When the sun shines on oceans, lakes, and rivers, the surface layer of water warms up. This causes it to **evaporate**, or turn into a **gas** called **water vapor** and rise into the atmosphere. As the water vapor drifts higher, it becomes colder. As it gets colder, it turns back into tiny droplets of liquid water that clump together to form clouds. When the liquid droplets become heavy, they cannot float in the atmosphere any longer, so they **condense**, or turn back into a liquid and fall as rain, snow, sleet, or hail.

The water that falls from the sky as rain is almost as old as Earth itself.

The rain, snow, sleet, or hail are types of **precipitation**. They fall into lakes, oceans, and rivers, or onto the land. When water falls on land, it either soaks into the surface or flows over the ground and collects in oceans, lakes, or rivers. Then the surface of the water warms up and the water cycle continues.

Get Smart!

Water is the only substance in the world that can exist as a gas (water vapor), liquid (water), and solid (ice) in the naturally occurring temperature ranges on Earth.

This diagram shows the water cycle. Water vapor rises into the air, forms clouds, and falls to the ground again.

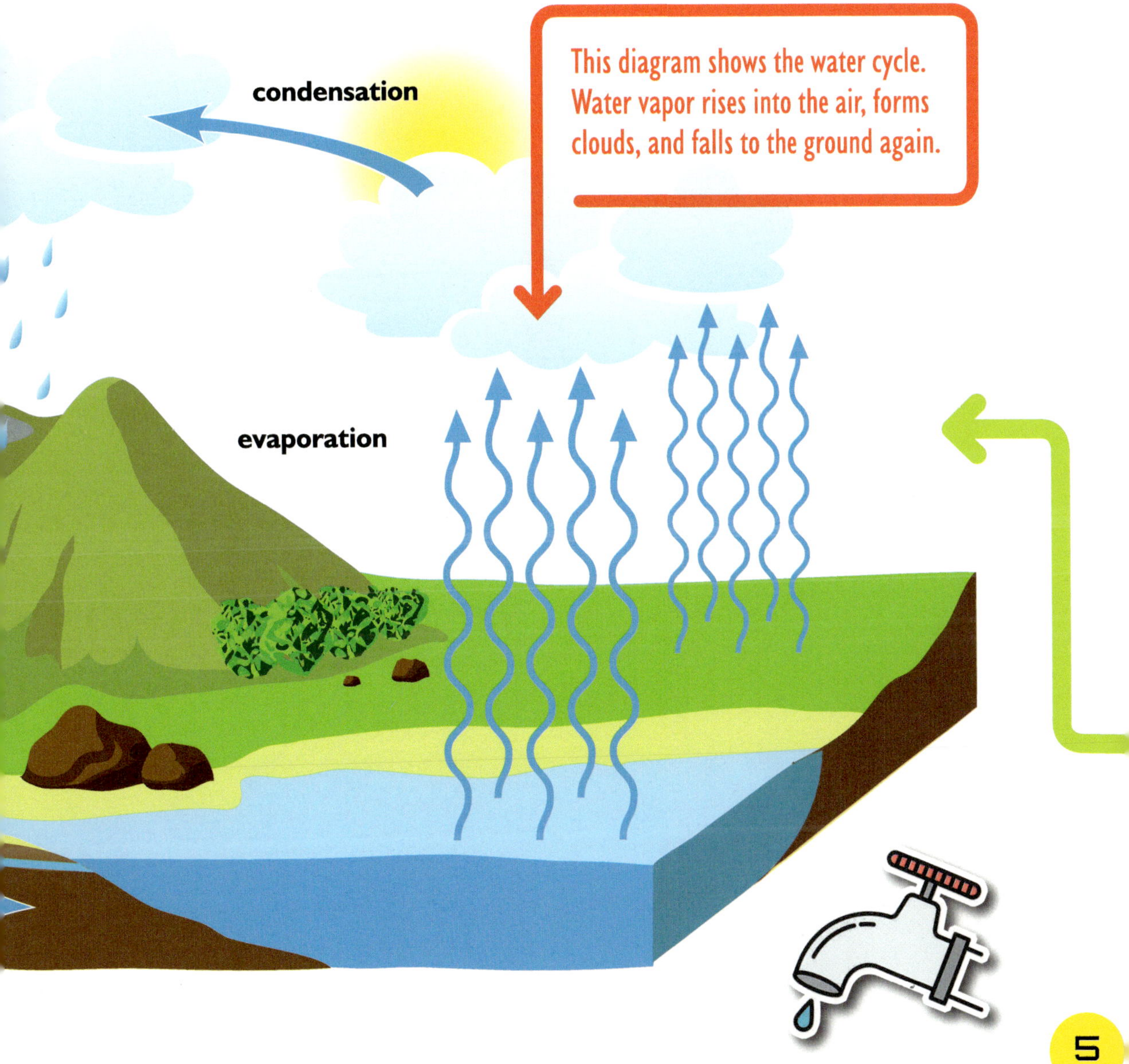

The Blue Planet

Earth is often called the blue planet because when viewed from space that is how it looks. Liquid water covers about 70 percent of Earth's surface. The water on our planet makes life possible. Without water, we and all the other living things on Earth, from the smallest plant to the largest whale, would not exist.

The water on Earth's surface is found mainly in the oceans. In fact, 97.25 percent of the entire planet's water is the salt water found in the oceans and seas. About 2.5 percent is freshwater, but most of this is trapped in the form of ice, such as in **glaciers**. Most of the rest is stored underground in what are called **groundwater** sources.

The five oceans of the world are all connected. Salty seawater flows between them.

Freshwater in lakes such as this one in Banff National Park, Alberta, Canada, flows in and out through streams and rivers.

We can only use freshwater because the salt in ocean waters makes it unsafe to drink. If an animal drinks salt water, its body is forced to urinate more to remove all of the extra salt. Eventually the animal's body dries out and it dies. In total, less than 0.8 percent of the world's water is actually freshwater that is available for humans to use and drink. This water is found in **reservoirs**, lakes, and rivers.

Get Smart!

During the water cycle, when ocean water changes into water vapor, it leaves behind the salt. This means that the water cycle **purifies** salt water. This creates freshwater for people to drink or use, and provides water for plants, trees, and crops.

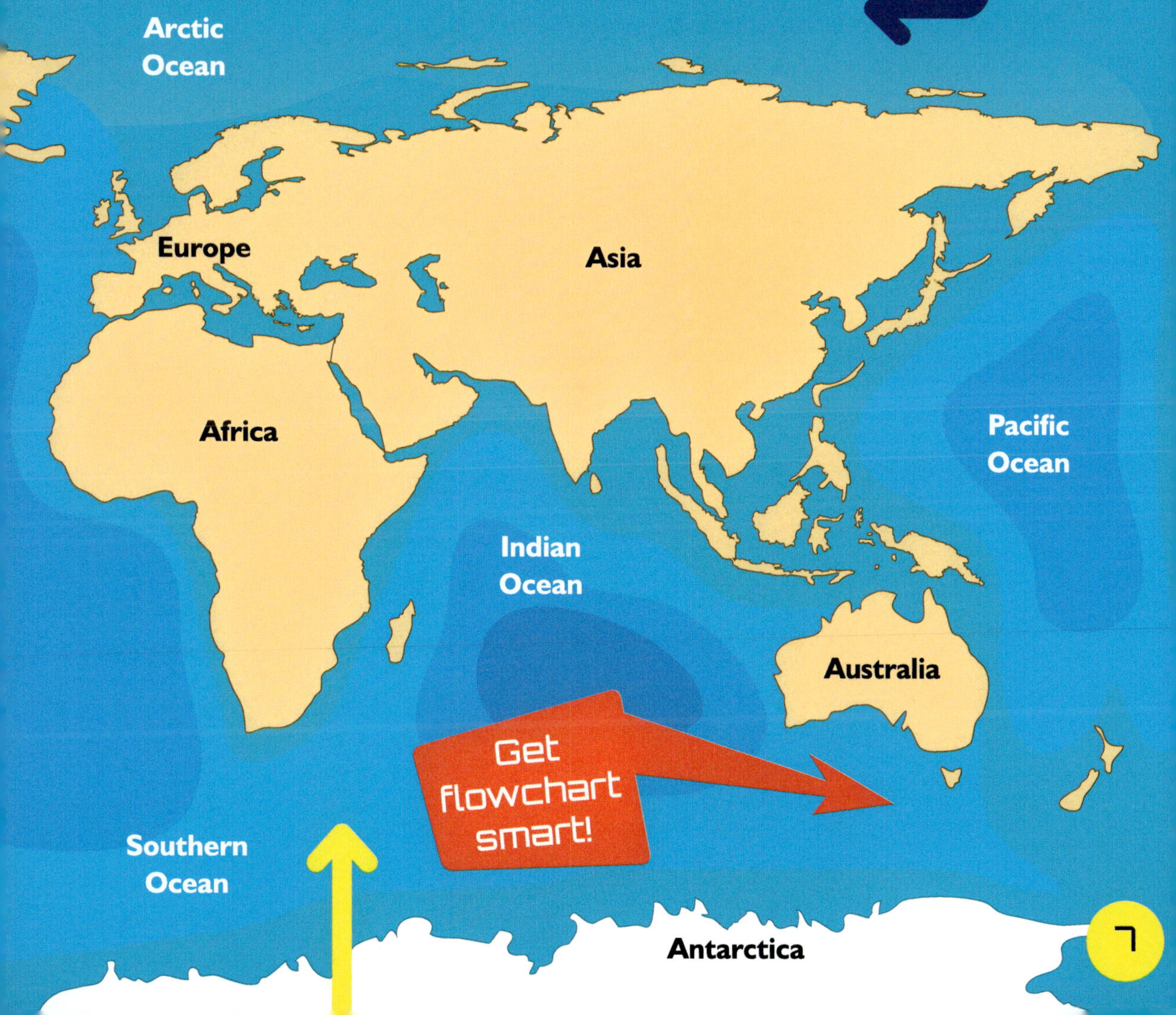

The Water Cycle in Action

Follow the steps in this flowchart to find out how water is recycled in the water cycle.

The sun shines down on oceans, lakes, and rivers. It warms the surface layer of the water.

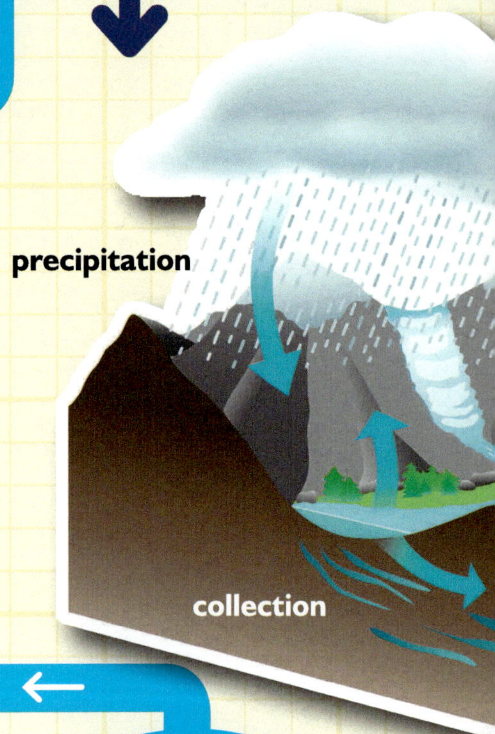

The rain, snow, sleet, or hail may fall into lakes, oceans, and rivers, or onto the land.

It collects in oceans, lakes, or rivers, warms up, and the water cycle continues.

Flowchart Smart

The warmth causes the surface layer of liquid water to turn into a gas called water vapor.

The water vapor rises up into the sky.

As the water vapor drifts higher, it cools down.

When the water vapor is cold, it turns back into tiny droplets of liquid water. The droplets clump together to form clouds.

When the water droplets in clouds become so heavy that they cannot float, they fall as rain, snow, sleet, or hail.

Chapter 2

Water in the Atmosphere

The atmosphere is a thick layer of gases wrapped around our planet. It protects Earth's surface by **filtering** out harmful rays from the sun. It also helps keep Earth at a suitable temperature for life to exist. The atmosphere contains water vapor, the gas form of water.

The atmosphere is made up of layers. The troposphere is the lowest layer of the atmosphere. It extends about 9 miles (14.5 km) above Earth. It contains almost 90 percent of the total amount of air in the atmosphere, and all its water vapor. The temperature of the troposphere varies and is colder the higher up you go. Above the troposphere is the stratosphere, which extends about 31 miles (50 km) above Earth's surface. Next lie the mesosphere and the thermosphere.

The sun is a star, but it is a very special star to us because it is close enough for its heat to spread into the troposphere. As it shines on Earth, it warms the planet's surface. Some of this heat bounces off the surface back into space. Some heat is trapped in the sky by gases in the atmosphere. These act like a blanket, keeping Earth warm. This is called the greenhouse effect because the gases trap warmth like glass in a greenhouse. The sun's heat is what powers the water cycle.

Water vapor is invisible. When vapor turns to liquid water we can see it as a cloud, fog, or mist.

The outer layers of the atmosphere extend upward toward space. The ozone layer is the region of the atmosphere that absorbs most of the sun's harmful rays.

Get Smart!

The atmosphere always contains roughly 3,120 cubic miles (13,000 cu km) of water. That is about as much water as there is in a large lake, such as Lake Superior in North America. It is enough water to cover the world in a layer about 1 inch (2.5 cm) deep.

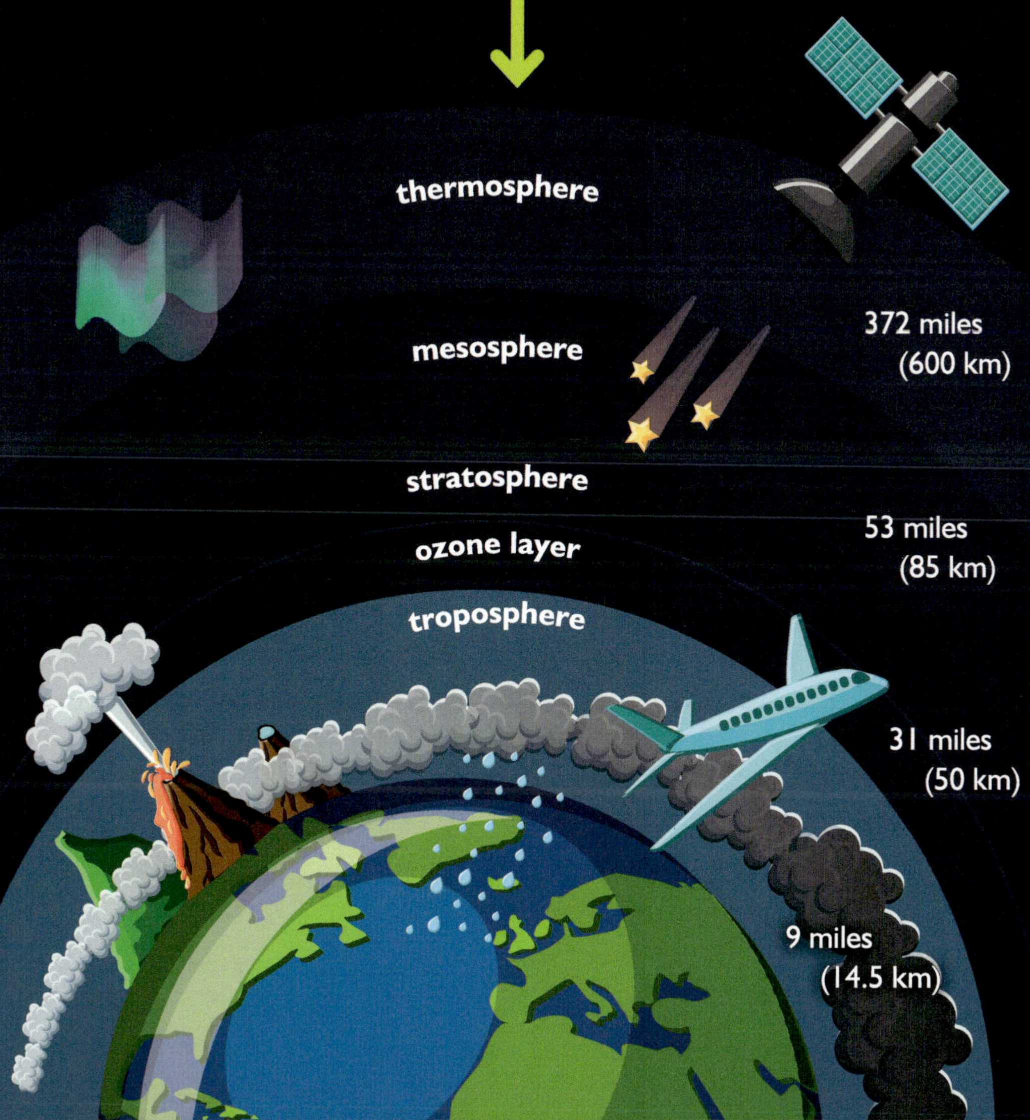

Evaporation in Action

All substances are made from tiny **particles**. The secret to why liquid water can evaporate, or turn from a liquid into a gas, lies in these tiny particles.

The particles that make up every substance in the world are called **atoms** and **molecules**. Atoms are incredibly tiny and are often described as the building blocks of matter. Molecules are made up of two or more atoms joined together. These particles are held together by pulling forces called **bonds**.

In a solid, the particles are tightly packed and bonded, usually in a regular pattern. The particles in a solid can **vibrate** a little, but they do not move from place to place. In a liquid such as water, the bonds between the molecules are less strong. The particles are still close together but not in a regular pattern. They can vibrate, move around, and slide past one another. That is why we can pour a liquid.

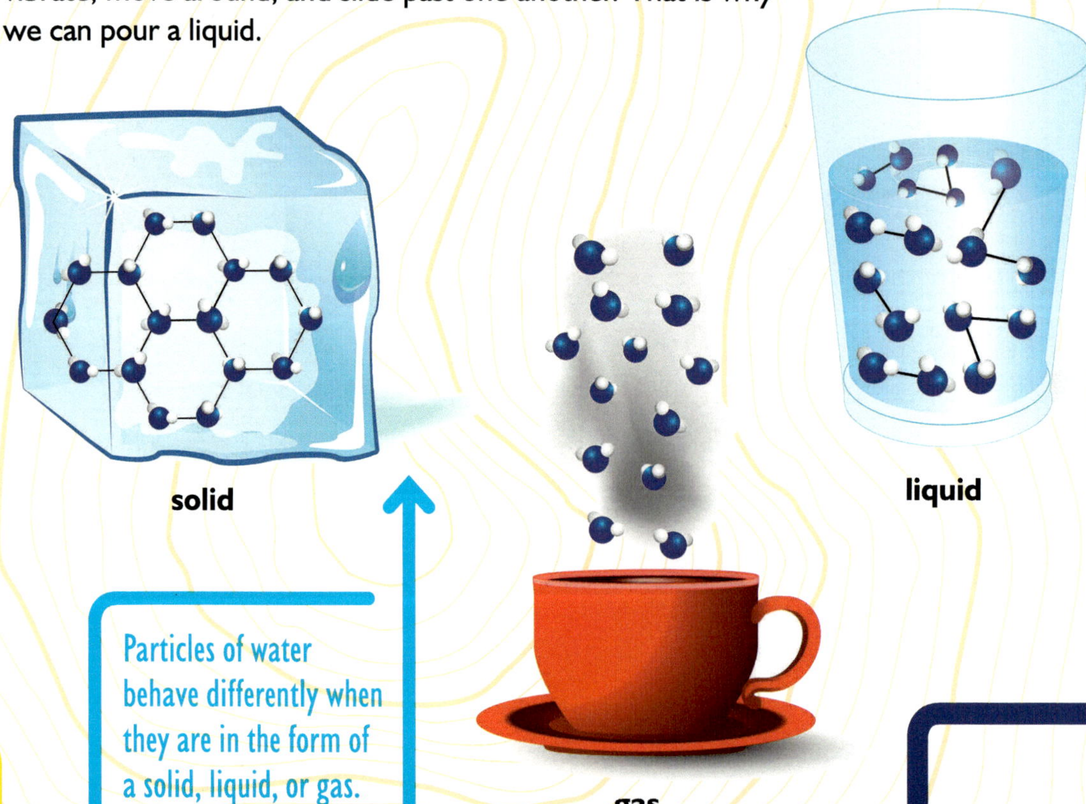

Particles of water behave differently when they are in the form of a solid, liquid, or gas.

When a liquid heats up, its particles move faster and faster. This causes some of the bonds between the particles to break. Some particles escape from the liquid as a gas. In a gas, particles vibrate and move freely at high speeds, so a gas can spread out in all directions. The change from a liquid to a gas is called evaporation.

Water evaporates from wet sheets when they are hung in warm air.

Get Smart!

Evaporation happens at the surface of a liquid. That is why the speed at which a liquid evaporates depends on the size of its surface area. A wide, shallow puddle evaporates more quickly than a narrow, deep puddle.

Get flowchart smart!

How Evaporation Works

Follow the flowchart for a closer look at evaporation.

The particles that make up liquid water are close together but in an irregular pattern. They can vibrate, move around, and slide past each other.

→

Some particles escape from the liquid as gas, or water vapor.

↓

In the water vapor, the particles vibrate and move freely at high speeds and in all directions.

Water vapor spreads out in the air above the water.

Flowchart Smart

When the sun shines down on Earth and heats surface water, the particles in the water move faster and faster.

When the water warms, the particles move so much that the bonds between them break.

Chapter 3

Water in the Clouds

Water vapor in the air spreads out and floats, but does not stay in one place. As the sun heats Earth's surface, this in turn heats the air above it. Warm air containing water vapor rises and drifts higher up into the sky. As the air moves higher into the troposphere, it cools. When the water vapor gets cold enough, it turns back into tiny droplets of liquid water. This process is called condensation.

Condensation is the opposite of evaporation. The particles in a gas are spread wide apart and are moving quickly in all directions. When a gas cools, its particles slow down. As they pass one another more slowly, bonds begin to form between the particles again. These bonds pull the particles closer together. When the particles are joined loosely together, the gas has become a liquid.

The droplets of water in a cloud are so small that 35 cubic feet (1 cu m) of air contains 100 million drops.

The tiny droplets of water that condense from water vapor float in the air. If the droplets become large enough, they may form clouds. The air is cooler the higher up you go, so clouds usually form high in the sky. Condensation of water vapor most often happens on the surfaces of cold, tiny fragments of smoke, dust, salt, or other particles in the air.

Get Smart!

When we breathe out, we breathe water vapor into the air around us. That is why when we step outdoors on a very cold day, we can see our breath as a "cloud." The cold air makes the water vapor in our breath condense into droplets that are large enough to see.

Our breath is warm and saturated with water. Cold air cannot hold as much moisture as warm air, so the water vapor condenses.

Falling Water

Condensation is essential to the water cycle. Condensation makes clouds form. These clouds may produce precipitation, such as rain, which is how water returns to Earth's surface in the water cycle.

There are three main types of cloud: cirrus, cumulus, and stratus. Clouds look white when the water droplets they contain are very small and tightly packed, so they reflect more light. Cumulus clouds are white and fluffy with flat bases. They form low in the troposphere on sunny days. It is gray clouds that bring rain. Clouds look gray because the water they contain has formed larger droplets. Larger water droplets reflect less light, so the cloud looks darker and gray. The bases of these clouds also look dark, because sunlight cannot easily shine through them. Stratus clouds look like gray blankets and bring fine, light rain.

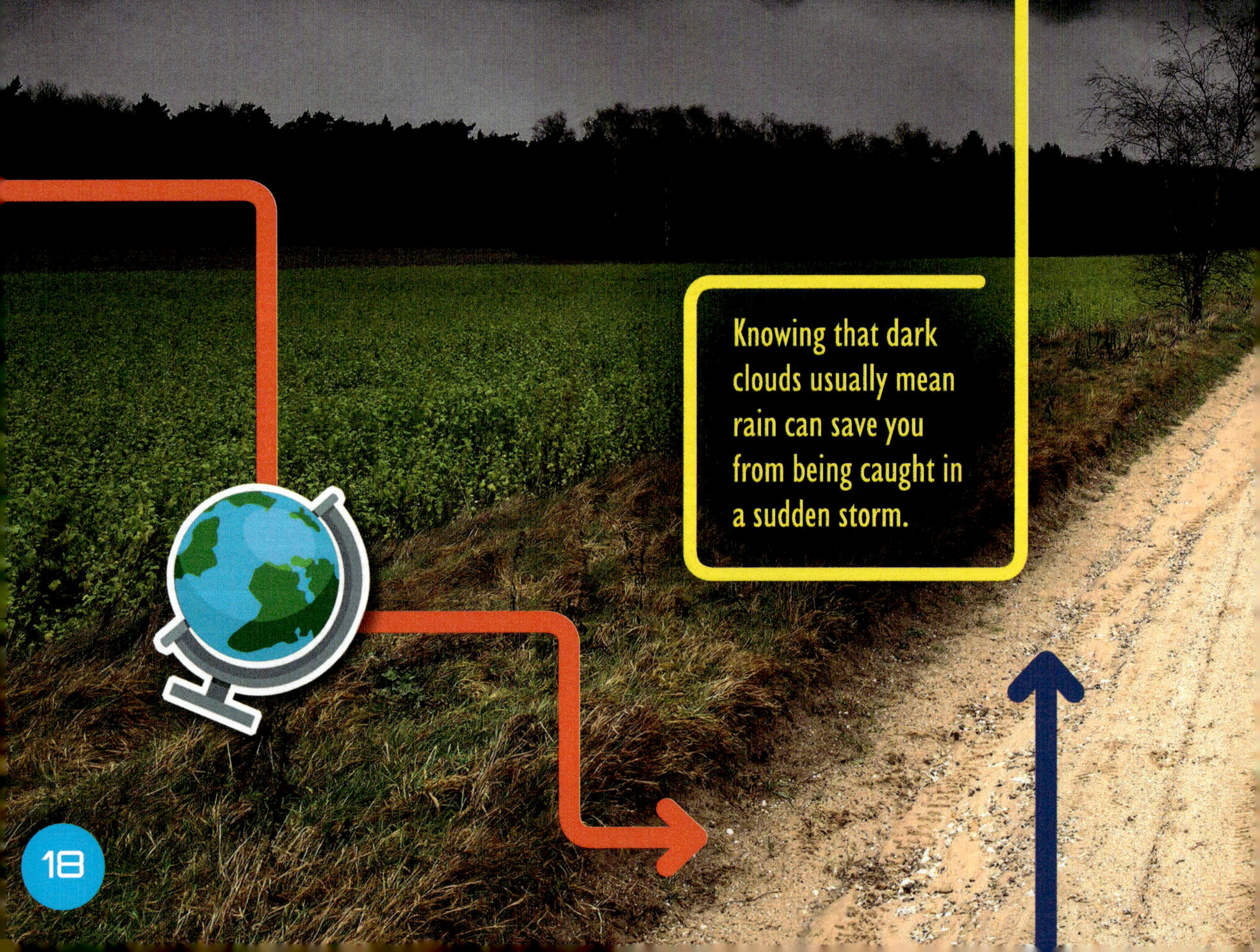

Knowing that dark clouds usually mean rain can save you from being caught in a sudden storm.

Small droplets in a cloud are constantly bumping into one another. As they do this, they join and form larger and larger droplets. Eventually, in some clouds, the droplets become too heavy to stay in the air. They are pulled down from the sky by the force of **gravity**. Many of the raindrops that land on Earth travel at speeds of almost 20 miles (32 km) per hour!

If raindrops grow any larger than 0.16 inches (4 mm) across, they usually split into two separate drops.

Get Smart!

Larger raindrops stay as liquid water as they fall through layers of warmer air on the way down to Earth's surface. Smaller, lighter raindrops may evaporate and turn back into vapor before reaching the surface, since they fall more slowly through the air.

Sleet, Snow, and Hail

Most precipitation falls as rain, but water released from clouds can also fall as sleet, snow, or hail. These forms of precipitation are important in the water cycle because they deliver water from the atmosphere back to Earth.

Water freezes when temperatures reach 32° F (0° C). Snowflakes form when tiny water droplets in clouds hit air that is cold enough to freeze them into small ice **crystals**. These crystals gradually join together to form snowflakes. Snowflakes that fall through very cold air stay frozen in their crystal form and reach the ground as snow. Sometimes, if the air is a little warmer, the crystals begin to melt, and then refreeze. This is called sleet. If snowflakes fall through even warmer air, they melt and fall as raindrops instead.

Sometimes, the crystals inside a cloud are blown up and down by powerful winds. As they are blown higher in the cloud where it is even colder, they become coated with a layer of ice and form hailstones. When they get blown down again, other water droplets attach themselves to the hailstone, and when it blows higher these droplets freeze onto the hailstone's surface. This is how small hailstones grow larger and larger. When hailstones are big and heavy enough, gravity pulls them down and they fall to Earth.

Every snowflake is unique. Each one has different numbers of crystals that grow in varying directions and shapes.

Get Smart!

On average, water stays in the air for about nine days before falling back to Earth's surface as some form of precipitation.

Most hailstones measure between 0.2 inch (5 mm) and 6 inches (15 cm) in diameter.

Get flowchart smart!

Condensation in Action

Follow this flowchart to see how condensation works in the water cycle.

When liquid water on Earth's surface evaporates into water vapor, it floats in the air.

As the particles pass each other more slowly, bonds begin to form between them. These bonds pull the particles closer together.

When the water particles are joined loosely together, the gas has become liquid water.

Flowchart Smart

Heat reflected from Earth's surface warms the air above it, causing the air to rise.

The particles in water vapor, a gas, are spread wide apart and move quickly in all directions.

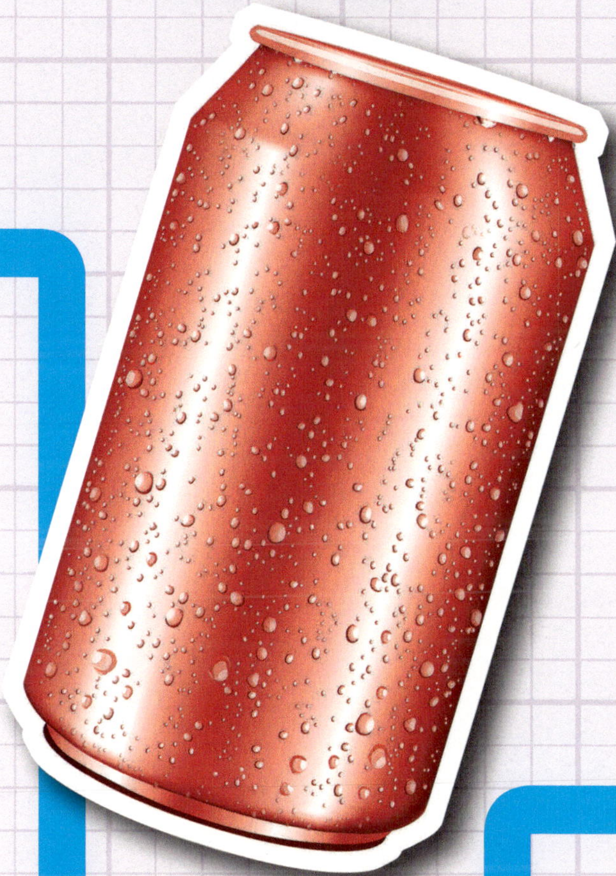

When a gas cools, its particles slow down.

Chapter 4

Water Stores

The four main stages in the water cycle are evaporation, condensation, precipitation, and collection. Collection is the process by which rain, snow, sleet, or hail is stored in the ground.

In the water cycle, there is much more water in storage at any one time than is actually moving through the cycle. When water is in storage, it stays in one place for a relatively long period of time.

Some precipitation becomes locked up as ice in ice caps and glaciers. These form when snow falls at the poles year after year. In warmer seasons, the temperature rises and the snow melts a little. When the temperature drops again in winter, the slightly melted snow freezes hard and is buried under new snowfall. The weight of snow presses down, making it more compact. After many years, the ice and snow layers fuse into a huge mass of solid ice called a glacier. It is extremely heavy and can slide very, very slowly into the ocean, where it may melt and become part of the water cycle again.

Glaciers store about 75 percent of the world's freshwater.

Most precipitation falls directly into the oceans. Precipitation that falls on land runs off the surface into creeks, streams, and rivers. This is called surface runoff. Surface runoff occurs when the ground cannot absorb any more water. This excess water enters streams, then flows into rivers, and eventually into the oceans.

If surface runoff passes over steep slopes or ledges of rock, it moves more quickly and forms a waterfall.

Get Smart!

Snowmelt is surface runoff that comes from melting snow. Snowmelt is a major part of the global movement of water in the water cycle. In colder regions, melting snow and ice causes much of the runoff in the spring.

Aquifers

Some of the precipitation that falls to Earth does not remain on the surface. Instead, it soaks into the ground to become groundwater. An aquifer is an underground area that stores water.

The water table is the level below which water can be found underground.

When rain or snowmelt soaks into the ground, this is called infiltration. Some types of land take water in more easily than others. Land that takes in water like a sponge is **permeable**. As the water moves underground, it passes through the soil and seeps through cracks and gaps in rocks. Some water is soaked up by the roots of plants and trees, but some flows farther downward until it meets a layer of less permeable rock. The water builds up and collects in an aquifer.

Almost all of the groundwater stored in an aquifer eventually flows back into the oceans, where it can once again travel as part of the water cycle. Water can leave an aquifer by seeping through permeable rocks to the ocean. Sometimes, an aquifer is so full that the water within it overflows onto the land surface through a gap in the rock called a spring. Other times, people pump groundwater out of the ground through wells.

Aquifers act as reservoirs for groundwater. Groundwater is the main source of drinking water for about one-third of the world's population.

Get Smart!

Some drops of water spend only a couple of months as groundwater in aquifers. Other water drops may spend around 10,000 years below Earth's surface.

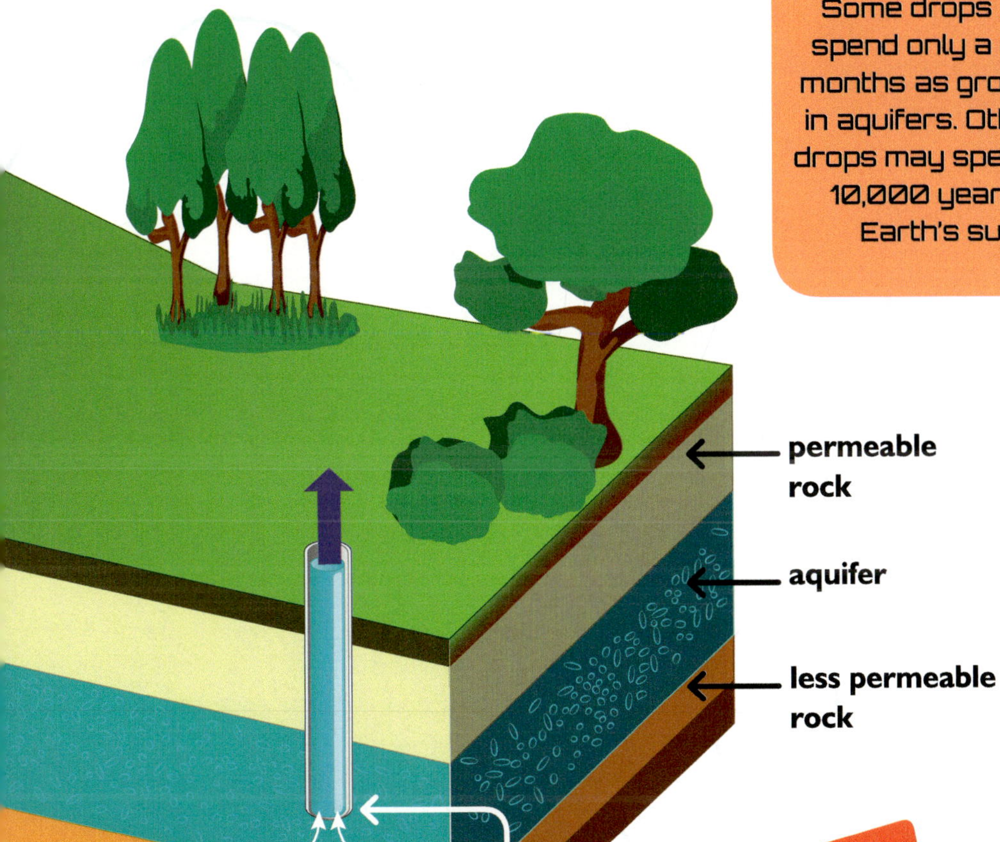

Get flowchart smart!

How Aquifers Work

Follow the steps in this flowchart to find out how aquifers work.

Precipitation falls to Earth. Some water soaks into the land.

If an aquifer is very full, water overflows onto the land surface through a gap in the rock called a spring.

Water can be pumped out of the ground from an aquifer through a well.

Flowchart Smart

The water passes through the soil and permeable rocks and seeps through cracks and gaps as it moves deeper underground.

The water flows downward until it meets a layer of less permeable rock.

Over time, water builds up and collects on top of the less permeable rock to become an aquifer.

Water often leaves an aquifer by seeping through permeable rocks. It eventually enters the ocean where it may evaporate as part of the water cycle.

Chapter 5

Water for Life

Water is the most important natural resource on our planet. It gives us, and every other living thing on Earth, life. It helps us keep clean and healthy, and provides us with food and even electricity.

Water makes up between 50 and 70 percent of a human's body weight. Water is found in saliva and blood, within body **cells**, and even in bones. Our body relies on water to function. The problem is that the human body cannot store water and we constantly lose water, for example when we urinate and sweat. We must drink water regularly each day to be sure we keep healthy. It is possible to survive for weeks without food, but only a few days without water.

In dry places, animals such as these zebras are constantly on the move to find freshwater.

Water is vitally important for keeping clean and healthy. Around two-fifths of the world's population do not have access to the clean water they need to wash, clean their homes, or dispose of **sewage** safely. This puts them in danger. Many diseases are spread by not washing hands with soap and clean, running water. **Diarrhea** can be deadly and dirty hands spread the germs that cause it. Handwashing reduces the number of people who get sick by one-third.

Get Smart!

Dehydration is when the body does not have enough water to function properly. Even being just a little dehydrated might make you feel tired and irritable, or give you a headache. If you lose more than 10 percent of your body's water, you are in danger. Serious dehydration affects the heart and kidneys, and can be fatal.

Keeping hands clean is one of the most important steps we can take to avoid getting sick and spreading germs to one another.

Water Power

Moving water contains a lot of energy. Just think about the power of the waves at the shore, or of a river rushing down a mountainside. Around the world, people harness the energy in moving water and use it to make electricity in hydroelectric power plants.

Most hydroelectric power plants are built on rivers. A large barrier wall called a **dam** is built across the river to create a reservoir of water behind it. Pipes allow some of the water to drop through the dam. This moving water turns a turbine, which is a machine with a bladed wheel that drives an electricity generator. Generators produce electricity.

Tidal power plants are usually built where a river meets the ocean. As the tide goes in and out, water flows through tunnels in a dam and turns a turbine. In other tidal power plants, the water flow is used to push air through a pipe, which turns a turbine that drives a generator.

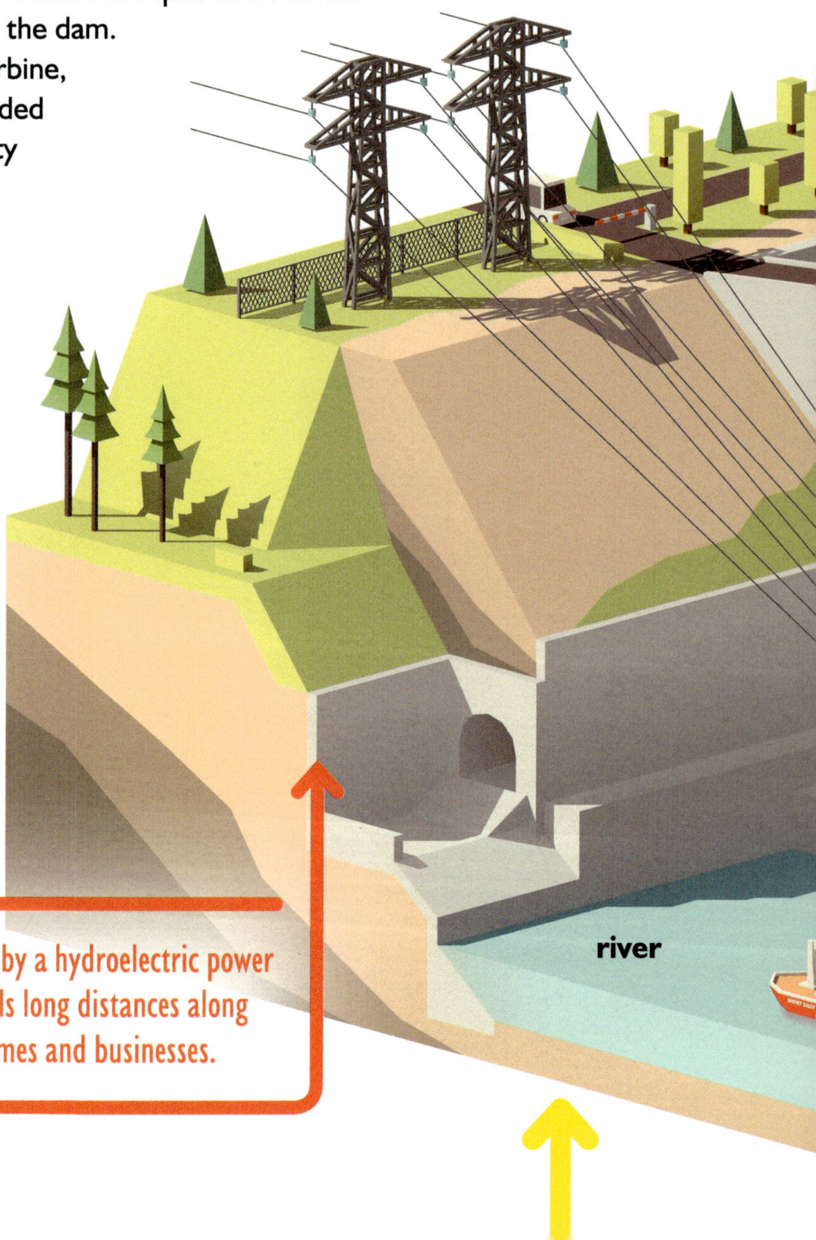

Electricity generated by a hydroelectric power plant at a river travels long distances along cables to people's homes and businesses.

Wind blowing across oceans creates powerful waves. At wave power plants, the water crashes in and out of a huge chamber of air. The air is forced in and out of a hole at the top of the chamber. This moving air turns a turbine inside the hole, which operates a generator.

Grand Coulee Dam is nearly 1 mile (1.6 km) long.

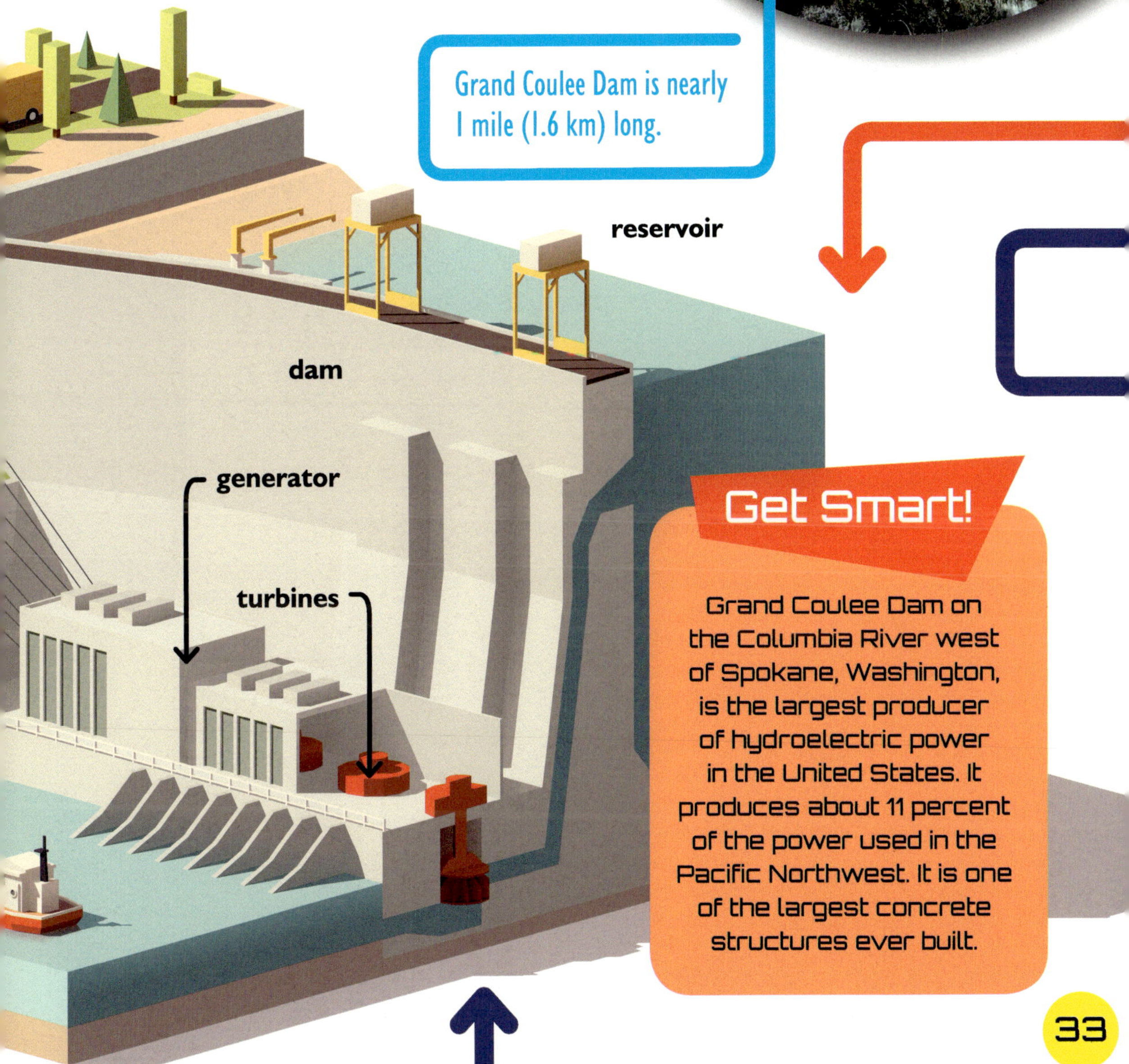

Get Smart!

Grand Coulee Dam on the Columbia River west of Spokane, Washington, is the largest producer of hydroelectric power in the United States. It produces about 11 percent of the power used in the Pacific Northwest. It is one of the largest concrete structures ever built.

Water and Food

Rainfall is vital for our survival. Rain and other forms of precipitation help plants grow. Without plants we would not have any food to eat.

Plants collect water through their roots. Roots are the parts of plants that grow underground. They anchor the plant in the soil and absorb, or soak up, water. This water is transported through the roots to the stems and up to the leaves. When the leaves warm up, small amounts of water evaporate through tiny openings on the leaves' surfaces called stomata.

As water escapes through the stomata, carbon dioxide enters the leaves, taking the water's place. This process is called **transpiration**. Carbon dioxide is a gas in the air. Plants use energy from the sun to combine carbon dioxide with water to make food, in the form of sugars. This process is called photosynthesis.

As well as providing humans with food, plants also provide other animals with food. Animals must eat plants, or animals that eat plants, in order to grow. When we drink milk or eat beef, we get energy from food that was stored in the grass and plants that the cow ate.

Plants are about 90 percent water. If it does not rain on a farmer's field, the farmer may irrigate, or water, his or her crops.

Get Smart!

Transpiration only occurs during the day when there is sunlight. Studies have revealed that about 10 percent of the moisture found in the atmosphere is released by plants through transpiration.

Without water, plants would not grow and produce delicious fruits such as strawberries.

Get flowchart smart!

Plants and Water

Follow the steps in the flowchart to find out how plants get water and use it to make the food they need to grow.

Plants absorb water from the soil through their roots.

Plants use energy from the sun to combine carbon dioxide with water to make food, in the form of sugars. This process is called photosynthesis.

Flowchart Smart

This water is transported through the roots, to the stem, and up to the leaves.

When the leaves warm up, small amounts of water evaporate through tiny openings on the leaves' surfaces called stomata.

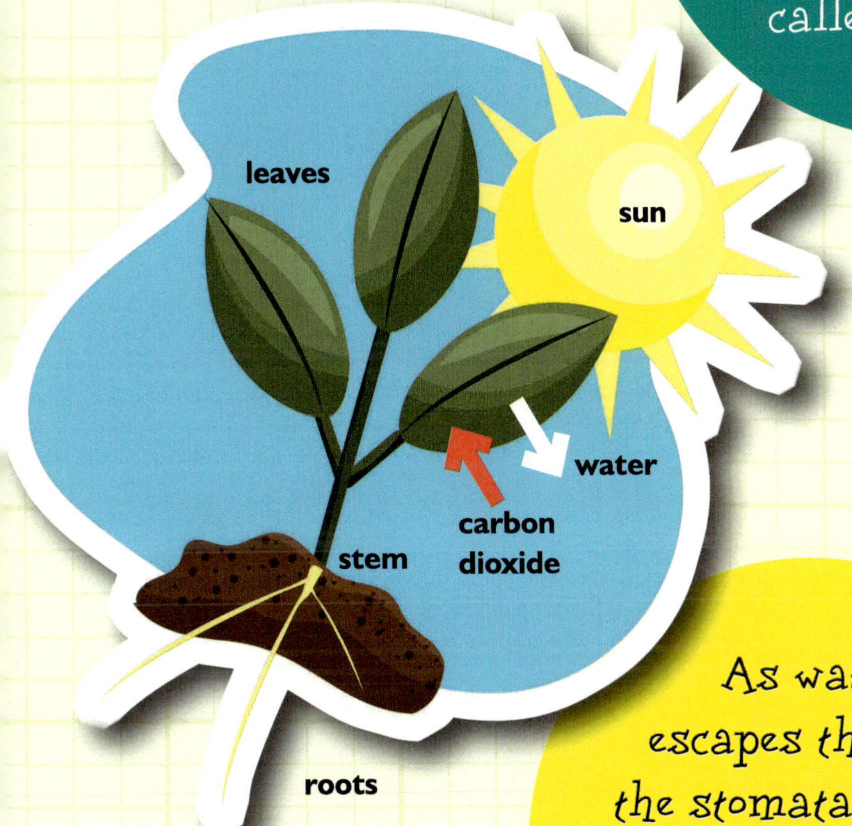

As water escapes through the stomata, carbon dioxide enters the leaves. This process is called transpiration.

Chapter 6

Using Water

There is the same amount of water on Earth now as there was millions of years ago. The same water goes around and around in the water cycle, between Earth and its atmosphere. There is a limited amount of water available to us, so we must be careful not to **pollute** it or overuse it.

The amount of water people use is increasing. This is partly due to the fact that the population is increasing. Every year, there are more people on Earth than there were before, all needing and using water. Industries also use more water every year, for example to produce goods such as food and paper, and to cool machines that make goods. Aquifers can dry up when people drain them faster than nature and the water cycle can refill them.

In developing countries, around 70 percent of factory waste is dumped untreated into waterways.

The other problem is pollution. In some countries, factories dump waste directly into rivers and oceans. Untreated sewage is also dumped into waterways. Chemicals such as **fertilizers** can run off fields into water sources. Other waste, such as gasoline from a car, can trickle into the ground and end up in the water cycle.

Get Smart!

Less than 1 percent of Earth's water is safe for drinking, and the amount of water used across the world is doubling every 20 years. Experts fear that by the year 2025, there will be a water crisis because the demand for water will exceed what is available by 56 percent.

Recycling Water

Nature recycles water as it travels through the water cycle. To clean water and make sure it is safe to use, people recycle water at a water treatment plant. Public drinking water systems use various methods of water treatment to provide safe drinking water for their communities.

The first step in water treatment is called coagulation. Chemicals are added to the water that cause the small particles of dirt in water to coagulate, or stick together. When they do so, they form larger particles that are easier to remove. They are removed by a process called sedimentation. The water is stored for a while until these large, heavier particles gradually sink and settle on the bottom.

Get Smart!

Many people buy drinking water in plastic bottles because they think it is cleaner, healthier, and tastes better. In fact, in most countries, water treatment plants ensure that tap water is perfectly safe to drink. If people do not like the taste of it, they can use a filtered water pitcher. This is less expensive and reduces the large amounts of energy required to make plastic bottles.

The water left behind after these large particles are removed looks clean, but it may still have tiny particles of dirt and other unwanted substances **dissolved** in it. To remove them, the water is passed through layers of different sized materials, such as sand, gravel, and charcoal. These act as filters and sift out dissolved particles, such as dust, **bacteria**, **viruses**, and chemicals. After the water has been filtered, a chemical is often added to kill any remaining bacteria and viruses, and to keep the water clean when it is piped to homes and businesses.

This water treatment plant cleans waste bath, sink, and washing water, known as gray water. It recycles the water so it can be reused.

Get flowchart smart!

Water Treatment

Follow the steps in this flowchart to learn how to filter, clean, and recycle water.

Chemicals are added to water to make small particles of dirt clump together to form larger particles. This is called coagulation.

A chemical is added to the water to kill any remaining germs and keep the water clean when it is piped to homes and businesses.

Flowchart Smart

The water is stored until the larger particles sink and settle on the bottom. This is called sedimentation.

The water that is left behind once the larger particles are removed is passed through layers of different-sized materials such as sand, gravel, and charcoal.

The layers of sand, gravel, and charcoal act as filters. They sift out particles, such as dust, bacteria, viruses, and chemicals.

Saving Water

Water is purified by the water cycle, but this process can take thousands of years. Water treatment plants can clean water more quickly, but it costs a lot to purify drinking water from polluted water sources. Water is a precious resource and we should do all we can to conserve it.

Rainwater is being collected from these roofs. It can be used for things like watering plants and flushing toilets.

Get Smart!

According to the World Water Organization, the average African family uses 5 gallons (19 l) of water each day, while the average American family uses between 100 and 176 gallons (380–670 l) of water each day.

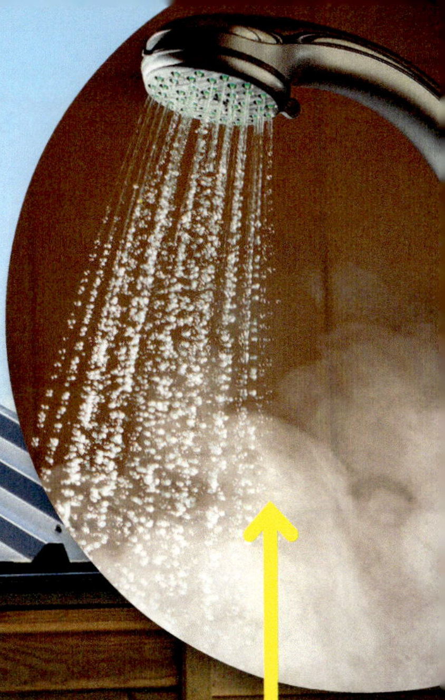

Conserve water by taking a short shower instead of a bath.

One way to conserve water is to use less of it. For example, be sure to turn off the faucet when brushing your teeth. Homeowners can install low-flush devices in their toilets and fix leaky faucets. Farmers and gardeners can use more efficient ways to water their plants. For example, watering plants during the early morning or evening saves water. When you water plants during the day, some of the liquid that lands on the surface evaporates before it can sink into the soil.

Governments make laws to reduce pollution and prevent industries and households from releasing certain types of waste into waterways. The Environmental Protection Agency (EPA) provides a list of cleaning and other products that will not pollute the water supply. Families can also make sure that they dispose of waste, such as old paint or motor oil, correctly and never flush old medication down the toilet. If we all do our part to save water, we can help keep the water cycle healthy for future generations.

Glossary

atmosphere The blanket of gases that surrounds Earth.

atoms Tiny particles that are the building blocks of all matter.

bacteria Tiny living things that can cause disease.

bonds Forces that pull or attract atoms and molecules toward one another.

cells Very small parts that together form all living things.

condense To cool and turn from a gas into a liquid.

crystals Substances that form in a regular, symmetrical arrangement.

dam A barrier built across a river.

dehydration The loss of too much water from the body.

diarrhea A condition that causes people to have frequent, watery bowel movements, which can cause dehydration.

dissolved When a solid has broken down and seems to have disappeared into a liquid such as water.

evaporate To change from a liquid into a gas.

fertilizers Chemicals farmers put on soil to help plants grow.

filtering Only allowing part of something to pass through.

gas A substance that is usually colorless and invisible, takes up space, and has weight, but has no shape or size of its own.

glaciers Slowly moving rivers of ice.

gravity A force that pulls objects toward Earth.

groundwater Water that has collected deep underground.

molecules Groups of atoms.

particles Tiny fragments of a substance.

permeable Describes a substance that allows liquids or gases to pass through it.

pollute To add dirty or harmful substances to the air, land, or water.

precipitation Water falling to Earth in the form of rain, snow, sleet, or hail.

purifies Makes clean and safe.

recycled Converted into something new.

reservoirs Lakes built by people to store water.

sewage Human waste.

transpiration The process by which water travels from roots to the leaves, where it changes to vapor, and is released into the atmosphere.

vibrate Move back and forth rapidly.

viruses Disease-causing particles that are too tiny to be seen by an ordinary microscope.

water vapor The gas form of water.

For More Information

Books

Amson-Bradshaw, Georgia. *Water Cycle Geo Facts*. New York, NY: Crabtree Publishing Company, 2018.

Heitkamp, Kristina Lyn. *The Water Cycle*. New York, NY: Britannica Educational Publishing, 2017.

Ransom, Candice. *Investigating the Water Cycle*. Minneapolis, MN: Lerner Publications, 2016.

Stewart, Melissa. *Water*. Washington, DC: National Geograpic, 2014.

Websites

Read about the water cycle basics at:
www.ducksters.com/science/the_water_cycle.php

Discover water cycle facts at:
www.eschooltoday.com/water-cycle/the-water-cycle.html

Find out how you can save water at:
www.nationalgeographic.com/environment/freshwater/water-conservation-tips

Explore an interactive water cycle diagram and more at:
water.usgs.gov/edu/watercycle-kids.html

Publisher's note to educators and parents: Our editors have carefully reviewed these websites to ensure that they are suitable for students. Many websites change frequently, however, and we cannot guarantee that a site's future contents will continue to meet our high standards of quality and educational value. Be advised that students should be closely supervised whenever they access the Internet.

Index

aquifers 26–27, 28–29, 38
atmosphere 10–11, 20, 38

clouds 4, 5, 9, 16–17, 18–19, 20
collection 24
condensation 4, 5, 9, 16–17, 18, 22–23, 24
conservation of water 44–45

drinking water 27, 30–31, 39, 40, 44

Earth 4, 6–7, 10–11, 15, 16, 18, 19, 20, 21, 22, 23, 25, 26, 28, 30, 38, 39
electricity, water and 30, 32–33
evaporation 4, 5, 9, 12–13, 14–15, 16, 19, 22, 24, 29, 35, 37, 45

food, water and 30, 34–35, 36
freshwater 6–7, 30

glaciers 6, 24
Grand Coulee Dam 33
greenhouse effect 10
groundwater 6, 26–27

health, water and 30–31
hydroelectric power plants 32–33

ice 6, 24, 25
infiltration 26

lakes 4, 5, 8
life, water and 6–7, 30–31, 32–33, 34–35, 36–37, 44
  human body 30–31
  plants 34–35, 36–37, 44

oceans and seas 4, 5, 6–7, 8, 24, 25, 26, 29, 32, 39

particles of water 12–13, 14–15, 16, 22–23
permeable rock 26, 27, 29
photosynthesis 34, 36
pollution 38–39, 45
precipitation 4–5, 8, 9, 18–19, 20–21, 24–25, 26, 28, 34, 44
  hail 4, 8, 9, 20–21, 24
  rain 4, 8, 9, 18–19, 20, 24, 26, 34, 44
  sleet 4, 8, 9, 20, 24
  snow 4, 8, 9, 20, 24, 25
  snowmelt 25, 26
  surface runoff 25

reservoirs 7, 27, 32
rivers 5, 6, 8, 25, 32, 39

salt water 6–7, 8
soil 26, 29, 36, 45
springs 26, 28
sun 4, 10, 11, 15, 16, 34, 35, 36, 37

temperature 4, 5, 9, 10, 13, 15, 16, 20, 23, 24, 37
  cooling 4, 9, 16, 23
  freezing 20
  warming 4, 5, 8, 10, 13, 15, 16, 23, 24, 37
tidal power plants 32–33
transpiration 34–35, 37

using water 38–39, 40–41, 42–43, 44–45

water, states of
  gas 4, 9, 10, 12–13, 14, 23
  liquid 5, 6, 9, 10, 12–13, 14, 16, 19, 22
  solid 5, 12
water cycle
  condensation, role of 18–19
  definition 4–5
  precipitation, role of 20
  quantity, stable 38
  recycling 8–9
  stages of 24
water table 26
water treatment plants 40–42, 43–43, 44
  coagulation 40, 42
  filters 41, 43
  sedimentation 40, 43
water vapor 4, 5, 9, 10, 14, 15, 16–17, 19, 22–23
wells 26, 27, 28